STO

ALLEN COUNTY PUBLIC LIBRARY

FRIENDS
OF ACPL

3 1833 00663 4296

W9-AHR-322

WHO'S THE FUNNY-LOOKING KID WITH THE BIG NOSE?

Copr. © 1958 United Feature Syndicate, Inc.

Peanuts® Parade Paperbacks

WHO'S THE FUNNY-LOOKING KID WITH THE BIG NOSE?

LIVE IT UP!
IT'S GOING
TO BE A
LONG WINTER!

Copr. © 1950, 1958 United Feature Syndicate, Inc.

Cartoons from *You Need Help, Charlie Brown*
and *The Unsinkable Charlie Brown*

by Charles M. Schulz

Holt, Rinehart and Winston / New York

"Peanuts" comic strips from *You Need Help, Charlie Brown*
Copyright © 1964, 1965 by United Feature Syndicate, Inc.

"Peanuts" comic strips from *The Unsinkable Charlie Brown*
Copyright © 1965, 1966 by United Feature Syndicate, Inc.

All rights reserved, including the right to reproduce this
book or portions thereof in any form.

Published simultaneously in Canada by Holt, Rinehart
and Winston of Canada, Limited.

First published in this form in 1976.

Library of Congress Catalog Card Number: 75-29870

ISBN: 0-03-017491-0

Printed in the United States of America

10 9 8 7 6 5 4 3 2 1

Comic strips to follow from *You Need Help, Charlie Brown*
Copyright © 1964, 1965 by United Feature Syndicate, Inc.

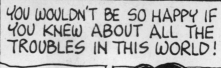

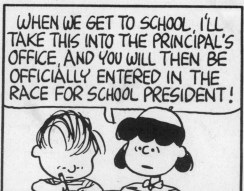

I ACCEPT THE NOMINATION FOR THE OFFICE OF SCHOOL PRESIDENT..

IF I AM ELECTED, I WILL DO AWAY WITH CAP AND GOWN KINDERGARTEN GRADUATIONS AND SIXTH GRADE DANCE PARTIES

IN MY ADMINISTRATION CHILDREN WILL BE CHILDREN AND ADULTS WILL BE ADULTS!!

I MAY EVEN DO AWAY WITH STUPID ELECTIONS LIKE THIS....THANK YOU..

I'VE DECIDED I WANT CHARLIE BROWN FOR MY VICE-PRESIDENT

OH, GOOD GRIEF!

WELL, WHAT'S **WRONG** WITH HIM? I THINK HE'D MAKE A **GOOD** VICE-PRESIDENT

MAYBE YOU'RE RIGHT..HE MIGHT EVEN HELP US WIN THE ELECTION

HE'LL PROBABLY BRING IN THE WISHY-WASHY VOTE!

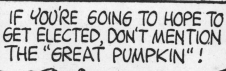

TO THE A.M.A.— GENTLEMEN, THIS IS A LETTER OF PROTEST WRITTEN WITH A SORE ARM.

YESTERDAY I WENT TO ONE OF YOUR DOCTORS, AND HE SAID I HAVE WASHER WOMAN'S ELBOW.

NOW, I ASK YOU. IS THAT ANY SORT OF AILMENT FOR A FUTURE MISS AMERICA?

GET ON THE BALL! SINCERELY, LUCY VAN PELT

I HAD TO SEE THIS FOR MYSELF...

MOM SAID YOU WERE EMPTYING THE WASTEBASKETS, AND SHE HAD TO ASK YOU ONLY TWICE..

SHE SAID THAT'S LIKE THE AVERAGE PERSON DOING IT WITHOUT BEING ASKED AT ALL!

I HAVE A VERY SARCASTIC MOTHER!

IS LUCY GOING TO PITCH AGAIN? IF SHE IS, I QUIT!

DO YOU KNOW WHAT SHE DID? SHE'S ALWAYS CALLING FOR CONFERENCES ON THE MOUND..

I GO OUT THERE, SEE...I GO OUT THERE FOR A SECRET CONFERENCE ON THE MOUND, AND YOU KNOW WHAT SHE DOES

SHE KISSES ME ON THE NOSE!

I'VE THOUGHT UP SOME STRATEGY FOR YOU, CHARLIE BROWN..

TELL THE OTHER TEAM WE'RE GOING TO PLAY THEM AT A CERTAIN PLACE THAT ISN'T THE REAL PLACE, AND THEN, WHEN THEY DON'T SHOW UP, WE'LL WIN BY FORFEIT!

ISN'T THAT GOOD STRATEGY?

I DON'T UNDERSTAND THESE MANAGERS WHO REFUSE TO USE GOOD STRATEGY!

SCHULZ

SNOOPY, I HAVE A SURPRISE FOR YOU...

SOME OF YOUR FRIENDS HAVE AGREED TO GET TOGETHER, AND GIVE YOUR HOUSE A REAL GOOD CLEANING...

WE'LL BE STARTING TOMORROW.. I JUST THOUGHT YOU'D LIKE TO KNOW...

JUST SO THEY DON'T DAMAGE MY VAN GOGH OR TEAR THE CLOTH ON MY POOL TABLE!

OKAY.. EASY NOW..

WATCH OUT... THERE'S A TURN HERE IN THE STAIRWAY..

DON'T DROP THEM, OR WE'LL HAVE GLASS ALL OVER EVERYTHING

DON'T YOU EVER RETURN ANY OF YOUR EMPTY POP BOTTLES?!

HOW EMBARRASSING!

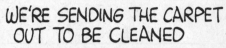

DEAR GREAT PUMPKIN, WELL, I WAITED, AND YOU DIDN'T SHOW UP.

IT'S A GOOD THING I'M YOUNG AND CAN STAND ALL THESE DISAPPOINTMENTS BECAUSE, FRANKLY, I'VE HAD IT!

THE ONES I FEEL SORRY FOR ARE THE OLDER PEOPLE WHO WAITED ALL NIGHT IN THEIR PUMPKIN PATCHES FOR YOU TO COME.

IF I SOUND BITTER, IT'S BECAUSE I AM.
SINCERELY,
LINUS VAN PELT
P.S. SEE YOU NEXT YEAR.

YOU'RE READING "THE BROTHERS KARAMAZOV"?

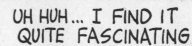

UH HUH... I FIND IT QUITE FASCINATING

DON'T ALL THOSE RUSSIAN NAMES BOTHER YOU?

NO, WHEN I COME TO ONE I CAN'T PRONOUNCE, I JUST **BLEEP** RIGHT OVER IT!

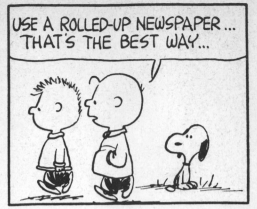

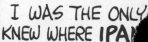

SCHULZ

CO. SCHOOLS
C854249

FOR THREE MONTHS I COUNTED THE DAYS UNTIL CHRISTMAS..

THEN LAST WEEK I STARTED TO COUNT THE HOURS...

THEN ON CHRISTMAS EVE I STARTED TO COUNT THE MINUTES; THEN THE SECONDS... I COUNTED EVERY SECOND UNTIL CHRISTMAS...

AND NOW IT'S ALL **OVER**!

FELICITAS EST PARVUS CANIS CALIDUS

THAT'S LATIN FOR "HAPPINESS IS A WARM PUPPY"

I CAN'T STAND IT!

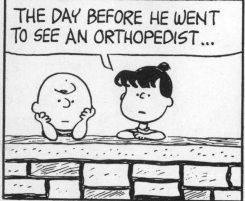

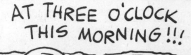

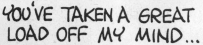

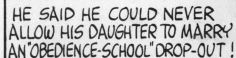

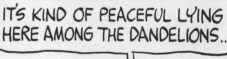

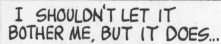

THROW THIS GUY YOUR FAST BALL, CHARLIE BROWN..

I THINK YOU'D BETTER KEEP THE BALL LOW TO THIS GUY, CHARLIE BROWN...GIVE HIM A LOW CURVE..

THROW THIS GUY ALL KNUCKLE BALLS, CHARLIE BROWN...YOU'LL FOOL HIM WITH KNUCKLE BALLS...

THIS IS THE LATEST THING... PITCHING BY COMMITTEE!

YOU GOT A "C" IN HISTORY? THAT'S ONLY AVERAGE!

SO WHAT? I'M AN AVERAGE STUDENT IN AN AVERAGE SCHOOL IN AN AVERAGE COMMUNITY....

WHAT'S WRONG WITH BEING AVERAGE?

BECAUSE YOU'RE CAPABLE OF DOING MUCH BETTER..

THAT'S THE AVERAGE ANSWER!

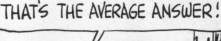

YOU THINK BEING AVERAGE IS ENOUGH, DON'T YOU?

WELL, IT ISN'T!

WHAT SHAPE WOULD THE WORLD BE IN TODAY IF EVERYONE SETTLED FOR BEING AVERAGE?

WHAT SHAPE IS THE WORLD IN TODAY?

IT'S JUST A LITTLE BRUISE... I THINK IT'LL BE ALL RIGHT...

DO I THINK IT'S GOING TO RAIN? NO, I DOUBT IT...THOSE DON'T LOOK LIKE RAIN CLOUDS TO ME..

SUPPERTIME? OH, YES...I THINK WE'LL BE FINISHED WELL BEFORE SUPPERTIME..

SOMETIMES I GET TO PITCH IN-BETWEEN QUESTIONS!

PERHAPS I WAS A BIT TOO OBVIOUS!

MISS OTHMAR?

SLURP SLURP

I WAS WONDERING IF YOU'D CARE TO RECONCILE OUR FAILURE TO SAY "GRACE" BEFORE DRINKING MILK WITH THE STORY OF DANIEL IN THE SIXTH CHAPTER OF THAT BOOK

OH...

MISS OTHMAR IS NEVER MUCH FOR RECONCILING...

SLURP SLURP

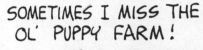

YOU'RE GETTING PRETTY GOOD ON THAT SKATEBOARD, LINUS!

BUT HE CAN'T DO "WHEELIES"!

IT'S JUST NO USE! I CAN'T PRACTICE WITH YOU HANGING AROUND!

THE TRUTH IS YOU'RE EMBARRASSED BY A PRETTY FACE! THAT'S IT, ISN'T IT?

A PRETTY FACE MAKES YOU UNEASY, DOESN'T IT? HUH? DOESN'T IT?!

HE SHOULDN'T FEEL THAT WAY... LOTS OF PEOPLE GET EMBARRASSED IN THE PRESENCE OF A PRETTY FACE...

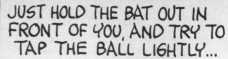

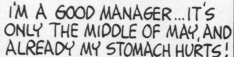

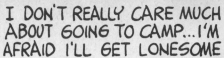

AS SOON AS SCHOOL IS OVER, I HAVE TO GO TO CAMP FOR TWO WEEKS..

I DON'T REALLY CARE MUCH ABOUT GOING TO CAMP...I'M AFRAID I'LL GET LONESOME

I'M AFRAID THAT WHEN I'M MILES AWAY FROM HOME, I'LL START TO MISS MY FRIENDS

WHAT FRIENDS?

IF YOU DON'T WANT TO GO TO CAMP, CHARLIE BROWN, WHY GO?

I FEEL OBLIGATED

MY MOM AND DAD THINK THEY'RE DOING ME A FAVOR...THEY'RE HAPPY BECAUSE THEY THINK THIS WILL BE A GOOD EXPERIENCE FOR ME

RATS!

POOR GOOD OL' CHARLIE BROWN...

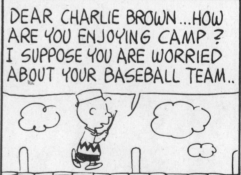

SNIF!

?

EXCUSE ME, BUT I COULDN'T HELP OVERHEARING YOU CRYING.. WHAT'S THE MATTER?

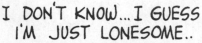

I DON'T KNOW... I GUESS I'M JUST LONESOME..

FRIEND!!

ROY, YOU'VE GOT TO SNAP OUT OF IT!

A CAMP LIKE THIS IS THE BEST PLACE FOR SOMEONE LIKE YOU...IT HELPS YOU TO BREAK THOSE OLD APRON STRINGS!

LIFE IS FULL OF EXPERIENCES THAT HAVE TO BE FACED ALONE!

BUT YOU SAID YOU WERE LONESOME, TOO..

I TALK A GOOD CAMP...

DEAR MOM AND DAD, THINGS ARE GOING BETTER HERE AT CAMP.

Yesterday I met this kid named Charlie Brown.

HE WAS VERY LONESOME, BUT I THINK I HAVE HELPED HIM.

He's the kind who makes a good temporary friend.

SCHULZ

C'MON, ROY, WE'LL BE LATE FOR THE "SING OUT"

WE'RE ALL GOING TO SIT AROUND THE CAMPFIRE, AND SING SONGS...

MAYBE I SHOULDN'T GO...

THOSE WORLD WAR I SONGS ALWAYS GET ME RIGHT HERE

SCHULZ

STRIKE THREE!

WHAT'S THE MATTER, KID? AIN'TCHA NEVER PLAYED BASEBALL BEFORE?!!

WHY DIDN'T YOU TELL HIM, CHARLIE BROWN? WHY DIDN'T YOU TELL HIM ABOUT HOW YOU'RE THE MANAGER OF A TEAM AT HOME?

SOMEHOW, MENTIONING A TEAM THAT HAS THREE GIRL-OUTFIELDERS AND A DOG-SHORTSTOP DIDN'T SEEM QUITE APPROPRIATE!

WELL, SO LONG, CHARLIE BROWN... IT'S BEEN NICE KNOWING YOU..

IT'S BEEN NICE KNOWING YOU, TOO, ROY....HAVE A GOOD TRIP HOME..

FOR THE FIRST TIME IN MY LIFE I FEEL I REALLY HELPED SOMEONE...HE WAS LONESOME, AND I BECAME HIS FRIEND...

WHAT AN ACCOMPLISHMENT!

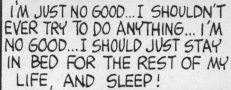

I STRUCK OUT, AND I LET MY TEAM DOWN...I'M NO GOOD FOR ANYTHING..

I'M JUST NO GOOD...I SHOULDN'T EVER TRY TO DO ANYTHING... I'M NO GOOD...I SHOULD JUST STAY IN BED FOR THE REST OF MY LIFE, AND SLEEP!

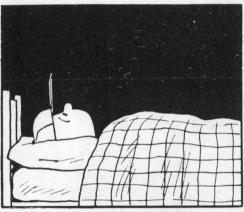

I CAN'T EVEN SLEEP GOOD!

YOUR TROUBLE, CHARLIE BROWN, IS THAT YOU LIVE BY MOTTOS AND TRITE SAYINGS..

YOU REALLY THOUGHT THAT IF YOU GRITTED YOUR TEETH IT WOULD HELP YOU TO BECOME A HERO.. WELL, THERE'S MORE TO LIFE THAN JUST GRITTING YOUR TEETH...

CHARLIE BROWN, DO YOU UNDERSTAND WHAT I'M TRYING TO TELL YOU?

MAYBE I DIDN'T GRIT THEM HARD ENOUGH...MAYBE IF I...

SIGH!

WHY DID YOU WRITE, "CHARLIE BROWN IS A BLOCKHEAD" ON THE SIDEWALK?

BECAUSE I SINCERELY BELIEVE YOU **ARE** A BLOCKHEAD! I HAVE TO WRITE WHAT I BELIEVE IS TRUE.. IT'S MY MORAL RESPONSIBILITY!

DEEP DOWN I ADMIRE HER INTEGRITY..

SCHULZ

I SUPPOSE I REALLY SHOULD TELL SOMEBODY..

BUT THEN AGAIN, WHY SHOULD I? IT'S MY SECRET...WHY SHOULDN'T I KEEP IT TO MYSELF?

IT'S KIND OF NICE HAVING A SECRET...

I'M THE ONLY PERSON WHO KNOWS THAT THERE ARE DOGS ON THE MOON!

SCHULZ

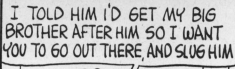

IT'S A GOOD THUMB, BUT NOT A GREAT THUMB!

SCHROEDER, DO YOU THINK I'M BEAUTIFUL?

I THINK YOU'RE THE MOST BEAUTIFUL GIRL THE WORLD HAS EVER KNOWN...

YOU HATE ME, DON'T YOU?

LISTEN TO THIS..

IT SAYS HERE THAT BY 1980 THERE WILL BE A NEED FOR 47,250 VETERINARIANS...

BUT IT ALSO SAYS THAT THERE WILL BE A SHORTAGE OF OVER 8000 VETERINARIANS...

REMIND ME NOT TO BE SICK IN 1980 !

SCHULZ

WHAT'S THIS ?

I HAVE HEARD THAT IT IS BETTER TO LIGHT A SINGLE CANDLE THAN TO CURSE THE DARKNESS

THAT'S TRUE..ALTHOUGH THERE WILL ALWAYS BE THOSE WHO WILL DISAGREE WITH YOU....

YOU STUPID DARKNESS!

SCHULZ

DEAR PENCIL-PAL, HAVE YOU HAD A NICE SUMMER?

I LIKE TO READ, DO YOU? I AM VERY FOND OF BOOKS.

I CAN ALWAYS ENJOY A GOOD BOOK. I HAVE ALWAYS BEEN THE SORT OF PERSON WHO ENJOYS READING.

WHEN I HAVE NOTHING ELSE TO DO, I READ.

SCHULZ

HOMEWORK ALREADY! WRITE A THOUSAND-WORD ESSAY ON WHAT WE DID DURING THE SUMMER!

NOBODY CAN WRITE A THOUSAND-WORD ESSAY ON WHAT HE DID DURING THE SUMMER! IT'S RIDICULOUS!

WHEN ARE YOU GOING TO TRY TO WRITE YOURS... THIS EVENING?

MINE'S ALREADY FINISHED...I WROTE IT DURING STUDY PERIOD!

YOU DRIVE ME CRAZY!!!

SCHULZ

DO YOU KNOW WHY ENGLISH TEACHERS GO TO COLLEGE FOR FOUR YEARS?

NO, I DON'T KNOW WHY ENGLISH TEACHERS GO TO COLLEGE FOR FOUR YEARS..

WELL, THEN I'LL TELL YOU WHY ENGLISH TEACHERS GO TO COLLEGE FOR FOUR YEARS....

SO THEY CAN MAKE STUPID LITTLE KIDS WRITE STUPID ESSAYS ON WHAT THEY DID ALL STUPID SUMMER!!

English Essay "What I Did This Summer"

I played ball, and I went to camp.

ONE, TWO, THREE, FOUR, FIVE, SIX, SEVEN, EIGHT....

NINE HUNDRED AND NINETY-TWO WORDS TO GO!

SCHULZ

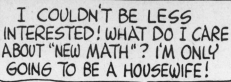

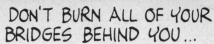

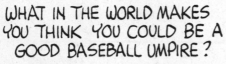

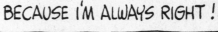

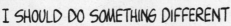

AN EYE PATCH? WHY IN THE WORLD SHOULD I PUT ON AN EYE PATCH?

BECAUSE I'M GOING TO TEST YOU FOR "LAZY EYE"... THIS IS ONLY A HOME TEST, BUT IT'S VERY IMPORTANT..

HERE, PUT ON THE EYE PATCH..

YO HO HO AND A BOTTLE OF RUM!

I'M WEARING THIS EYE PATCH SO YOU CAN TEST ME FOR WHAT?

FOR "AMBLYOPIA EX ANOPSIA" OR WHAT IS CALLED "LAZY EYE"

"AMBLYOPIA" REFERS TO DIMNESS OF VISION, AND "EX ANOPSIA" TO THE LACK OF USE WHICH IS RESPONSIBLE FOR THE DIMNESS OF VISION

ARE YOU SURE THIS DOESN'T HAVE SOMETHING TO DO WITH THE "NEW MATH"?

OH, GOOD GRIEF!

ONLY 6 DAYS UNTIL BEETHOVEN'S BIRTHDAY

ELEVEN DAYS TO THE FIRST DAY OF WINTER

ONLY 12 SHOPPING DAYS UNTIL CHRISTMAS

IT'S UNUSUAL FOR ONE AGENCY TO HAVE ALL THREE ACCOUNTS!

MOMS SAYS TO GET STARTED ON YOUR HOMEWORK

TELL HER I'M CONDUCTING AN EXPERIMENT TO SEE WHAT WOULD HAPPEN TO SOMEONE WHO NEVER DID HIS HOMEWORK, BUT JUST SAT AND WATCHED TV EVERY EVENING...

MOM SAYS TO GET STARTED ON THAT HOMEWORK RIGHT NOW!

I SHOULD THINK THE RESULTS OF SUCH AN EXPERIMENT COULD PROVE TO BE QUITE VALUABLE...

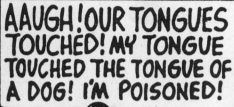

Comic strips to follow from *The Unsinkable Charlie Brown*
Copyright © 1965, 1966 by United Feature Syndicate, Inc.

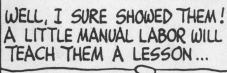

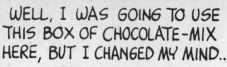

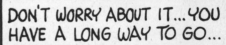

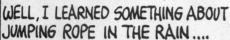
WELL, I LEARNED SOMETHING ABOUT JUMPING ROPE IN THE RAIN....

SOME JUMP ROPES **SHRINK** !

R R R R R R

THAT VACUUM CLEANER SURE MAKES A LOT OF NOISE...

R R R R R

R R R R R R R R R R

YOU'D MAKE A LOT OF NOISE TOO IF SOMEONE WERE PUSHING YOU ACROSS A CARPET ON YOUR FACE!

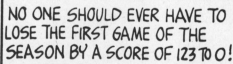

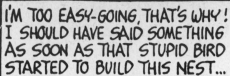

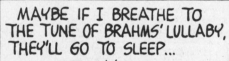

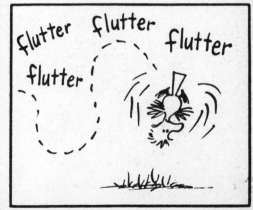

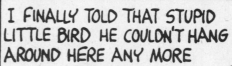

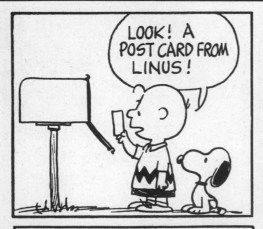

DON'T TELL ME I'VE GROWN ACCUSTOMED TO **THAT** FACE!

CLOMP HEY!

YOU GOT THE WRONG GUY! I'M NOT LINUS! LINUS HAS MOVED AWAY! HE JUST LEFT ME HIS BLANKET! STOP! STOP, I SAY!

MY APOLOGIES

STUPID DOG!!

 SO HERE I AM AT CAMP, LYING IN MY BUNK

 I HOPE NO QUEEN SNAKES CRAWL IN HERE DURING THE NIGHT...

 WHAT IF MY MOTHER AND DAD MOVE AWAY WHILE I'M GONE, AND DON'T TELL ME?

 HI! MY NAME IS ROY...HOW ARE YOU DOING?

OH, I'M DOING ALL RIGHT, I GUESS...

 YOU'LL GET TO LIKE THIS CAMP AFTER A FEW DAYS...I WAS HERE LAST YEAR, AND I THOUGHT I'D NEVER MAKE IT, BUT I DID...

OH?

 YOU KNOW WHAT HAPPENED? I MET THIS FUNNY ROUND-HEADED KID...I CAN'T REMEMBER HIS NAME.. HE SURE WAS A FUNNY KID...

 HE WAS ALWAYS TALKING ABOUT THIS PECULIAR DOG HE HAD BACK HOME, AND SOME NUTTY FRIEND OF HIS WHO DRAGGED A BLANKET AROUND

THAT BLANKET! YOU'RE THE ONE THAT ROUND-HEADED KID WAS TELLING ME ABOUT!

BOY, YOU'D BETTER PUT THAT BLANKET AWAY...IF THE OTHER KIDS SEE IT, THEY'LL TEASE YOU RIGHT OUT OF CAMP!

CRACK!

THEY WON'T TEASE ME MORE THAN ONCE...

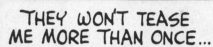

Dear Linus, How are things at camp?

I almost made you some cookies today, but then I thought, "Why bother?"

Instead, I went out and bought some, but they looked so good I ate them all myself.

Have a nice time at camp. Your sister, Lucy

C'MON, LINUS, EACH OF US IS SUPPOSED TO SAY A FEW WORDS AROUND THE CAMPFIRE TONIGHT...

AS I STAND HERE TONIGHT FAR FROM HOME, I AM REMINDED OF THE WORDS FROM JEREMIAH, "KEEP YOUR VOICE FROM WEEPING, AND YOUR EYES FROM TEARS;

FOR YOUR WORK SHALL BE REWARDED, SAYS THE LORD, AND THEY SHALL COME BACK FROM THE LAND OF THE ENEMY. THERE IS HOPE FOR THE FUTURE, SAYS THE LORD, AND YOUR CHILDREN SHALL COME BACK TO THEIR OWN COUNTRY."

INCIDENTALLY, HAVE ANY OF YOU EVER BEEN TOLD ABOUT "THE GREAT PUMPKIN"?

LOOK, LUCY, I GOT A LETTER FROM LINUS!

THAT BLOCKHEAD! HE NEVER WROTE TO ME!

HE SAID HE'S MET ROY, THAT SAME KID I MET LAST YEAR... AND HE SAID HE GAVE A LITTLE TALK AROUND THE CAMPFIRE LAST NIGHT

THAT STUPID BLOCKHEAD

HE SAID HE TOLD ALL THE KIDS ABOUT "THE GREAT PUMPKIN," AND AFTERWARDS THEY ELECTED HIM CAMP PRESIDENT!

HE SAID HE'S GOING TO STAY FOR AN EXTRA WEEK, AND TO GREET EVERYONE BACK HERE...

HE WROTE TO YOU, BUT HE DIDN'T WRITE TO ME! THAT BLOCKHEAD!

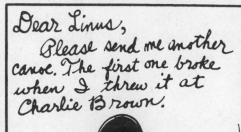

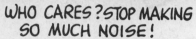

Panel 1: LET'S HUSTLE A LITTLE MORE ON THOSE FLY-BALLS!

Panel 2: C'MON! MOVE IN ON THOSE GROUNDERS! THROW THE BALL! DON'T HANG ON TO IT!

Panel 3: ALL RIGHT! EVERYBODY OVER HERE ON THE DOUBLE! LET'S GO!

Panel 4: OKAY, TEAM, THIS IS THE START OF A NEW SEASON, AND I HAVE A FEW WORDS TO SAY..

Panel 5: NOW, I THINK NO ONE WILL DENY THAT SPIRIT PLAYS AN IMPORTANT ROLE IN WINNING BALL GAMES..

Panel 6: SOME MIGHT SAY THAT IT PLAYS THE MOST IMPORTANT ROLE..

Panel 7: THE DESIRE TO WIN IS WHAT MAKES A TEAM GREAT.. WINNING IS EVERYTHING!

Panel 8: THE ONLY THING THAT MATTERS IS TO COME IN FIRST PLACE!

Panel 9: WHAT I'M TRYING TO SAY IS THAT NO ONE EVER REMEMBERS WHO COMES IN SECOND PLACE!

Panel 10: I DO, CHARLIE BROWN... IN 1928, THE GIANTS AND PHILADELPHIA FINISHED SECOND.. IN 1929, IT WAS PITTSBURGH AND THE YANKEES.. IN 1930, IT WAS CHICAGO AND WASHINGTON.. IN 1931, IT WAS THE GIANTS AND THE YANKEES.. IN 1932, IT WAS PITTSBURGH AND...

Panel 11: AND ANOTHER GREAT SEASON GETS UNDERWAY!

SCHULZ

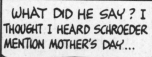

GOOD GRIEF! ANOTHER HOME RUN!

BOY, I MUST BE STUPID TO STAND OUT HERE, AND TAKE A BEATING LIKE THIS!

MY TEAM HATES ME, I'M A LOUSY PITCHER, MY STOMACH HURTS...... I DON'T KNOW WHY I PLAY THIS GAME..I MUST REALLY BE STUPID!

CHARLIE BROWN, YOU CAN'T GO ON LIKE THIS..YOU'VE GOT TO CHANGE YOUR ATTITUDE! THE YEARS ARE GOING BY, AND YOU'RE NOT ENJOYING LIFE AT ALL!

JUST REMEMBER, CHARLIE BROWN... THE MOMENTS YOU SPEND OUT HERE ON THIS PITCHER'S MOUND ARE MOMENTS TO BE TREASURED!

WE'RE NOT GOING TO BE KIDS FOREVER, CHARLIE BROWN, SO TREASURE THESE MOMENTS...

POW!

THIS IS A DIFFICULT MOMENT TO TREASURE!

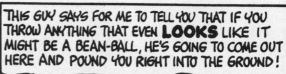

THIS GUY SAYS FOR ME TO TELL YOU THAT IF YOU THROW ANYTHING THAT EVEN **LOOKS** LIKE IT MIGHT BE A BEAN-BALL, HE'S GOING TO COME OUT HERE AND POUND YOU RIGHT INTO THE GROUND!

POW!

I THINK THEY'RE BEGINNING TO GET TO ME...I NEED A NEW PITCH OR SOMETHING...WHAT DO YOU THINK I NEED, SCHROEDER?

A CONCRETE PILLBOX!

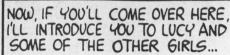

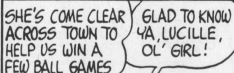

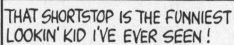
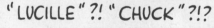

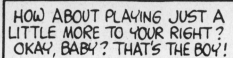

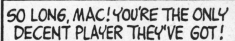